PIANO • VOCAL SELECTIONS

R&H THEATRICALS
229 West 28th Street, 11th Floor
New York, New York 10001
Tel 800/400.8160 or 212/564.4000 * Fax 212/268.1245 * E-mail theatre@rnh.com
www.rnh.com

ISBN 978-0-88188-059-5

AN IMAGEM COMPANY™
www.williamsonmusic.com

Contents

ALL AT ONCE

Words by LORENZ HART
Music by RICHARD RODGERS

Cmaj7 G7♯5 C Dm/C B/C C C/B Am7 G(♭5)/D G/D
sense. If you think I'm still a ba - by Then you must
a tempo
A7♭5 A7 Dm7 D7 Am7 Adim7 Am7/D D7 G
be dense. All at once
rit.
a tempo
C/G G B♭dim7 D7 Ddim7 Am7 D9 D7♭9 G
Ba - by starts in tod - dling. And all at once
C/G G B♭dim7 D7 Ddim7 Am7 D9 D7♭9 G G7
Ba - by needs no cod - dling. Then soon

Cmaj13
Am7
D13
4fr
Bm7
Knows all the names
Of toys and games,
Bdim
E7
E7sus
A7
Am7
D7
Dis - cov - ers bliss in
kiss - in'!
G
Am
G
C/G
G
B♭dim7
D7
Ddim7
All at once
Ba - by needs af -
Am7
D9
4fr
D7♭9
4fr
G
Am
G
C/G
G
B♭dim7
D7
Ddim7
fec - tion
To fall at once
In the right di -

Slower

Am7 D9 D7♭9 Gmaj7 G7 C Bdim7 Am

rec - tion. If you were wise, Or had eyes,

Dm7 G9 Cmaj7 C♯dim7 G/D Edim7

You'd be a - ble to see All at once

rit. *a tempo*

D7 G E♭7

Ba - by's goin' to love me.

A♭ B♭m A♭ D♭ A♭/C Bdim7 E♭7 Adim7

All at once Ba - by needs af -

B♭m7
D♭/E♭
E♭7♭9
A♭
B♭m
A♭
D♭
A♭/C
Bdim7
fec - tion To fall at once
E♭7
Adim7
B♭m7
E♭9
E♭7♭9
A♭maj7
A♭7
In the right di - rec - tion. If you were wise,
D♭
Cdim7
B♭m
E♭m7
A♭9
D♭maj7
Ddim7
Or had eyes, You'd be a - ble to see
3
A♭/E♭
D♭/E♭
A♭/E♭
Fdim7
E♭7
A♭
All at once Ba - by's goin' to love me.
rall.

BABES IN ARMS

Words by LORENZ HART
Music by RICHARD RODGERS

Cmaj7 C6 C♯dim7 G7 C♯dim7

Babes in arms, ___ But we'll be laugh - ing

G7 G7sus G7 C Cmaj7 C6

far more. ___ On cit - y streets and farms ___

sempre poco a poco cresc.

C♯dim7 G7 C♯dim7 G7 D♯dim7

___ They'll hear a ris - ing war cry. ___

C Dm7 D♯dim7 C/E Fmaj7

Youth will ar - rive, Let them know you're a - live, make it your ___

mf *cresc. molto*

f

G7
C
Cmaj7
cry
They call us Babes in
mp
C6
Cmaj7
Dm7
G7
Dm
arms,
They think they must di - rect us.
G7
C
Cmaj7
C6
C#dim7
But if we're Babes in arms,
G7
C#dim7
G7
G7sus
G7
C
We'll make them all re - spect us.
Why have we
sempre

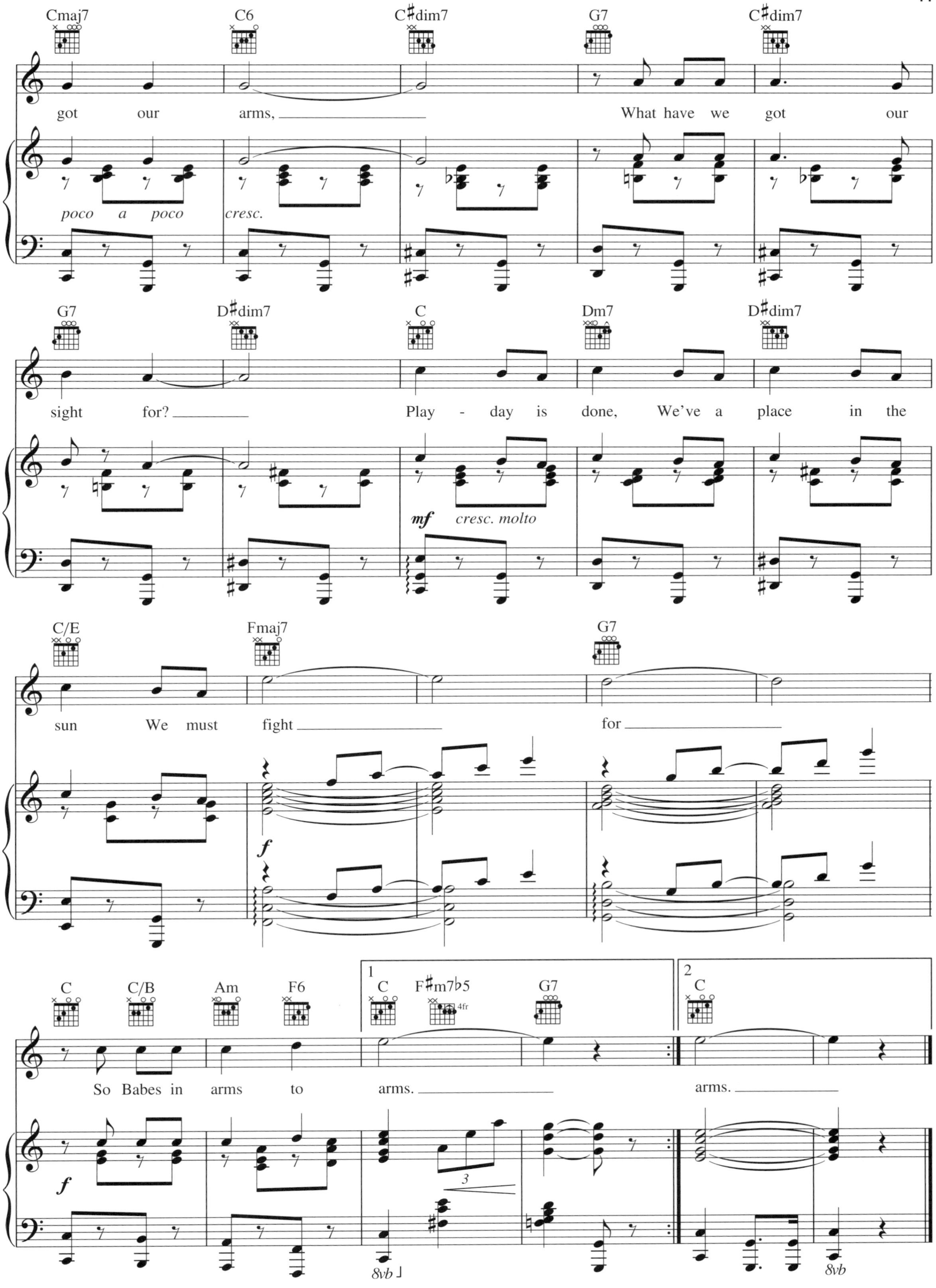
Cmaj7
C6
C♯dim7
G7
C♯dim7
got our arms,
What have we got our
poco a poco cresc.
G7
D♯dim7
C
Dm7
D♯dim7
sight for?
Play - day is done, We've a place in the
mf cresc. molto
C/E
Fmaj7
G7
sun We must fight
for
f
C
C/B
Am
F6
1
C
F♯m7♭5
4fr
G7
2
C
So Babes in arms to arms.
arms.
f
3
8vb
8vb

I WISH I WERE IN LOVE AGAIN

Words by LORENZ HART
Music by RICHARD RODGERS

Em7
A7
D9
4fr
D7
G
C/E
A7
Ap - pe - tite and health re - stored. You don't know how much I'm
D7
G♯dim7
D7/A
G
bored! The sleep - less nights, The
(The) fur - tive sigh, The
mf
Gdim7
G
Gdim7
dai - ly fights, The quick to - bog - gan when you reach the heights; I
black - ened eye, The words, "I'll love you till the day I die," The
G
Gdim7
D7/A
B♭dim7
miss the kiss - es and I miss the bites, I wish I were in
self - de - cep - tion that be - lieves the lie, I wish I were in

D7sus/A
D7
G
Gdim7
love a - gain! The bro - ken dates, The end - less waits, The
love a - gain! When love con - geals It soon re - veals The
G
Gdim7
G
love - ly lov - ing and the hate - ful hates, The con - ver - sa - tion with the
faint a - ro - ma of per - form - ing seals, The dou - ble cross - ing of a
Gdim7
D7
G7
fly - ing plates, I wish I were in love a - gain!
pair of heels, I wish I were in love a - gain!
C
Cm
3fr
G/B
E7♯5(♭9)
6fr
A7
D7
G
G7
No more pain, No more strain,
No more care, No de - spair.

C Cm G/B E7♯5(♭9) A7
3fr
6fr
Now I'm sane, but I would rath - er be
I'm all there now, But I'd rath - er be
D9 D7 G Gdim7
4fr
ga - ga! The pulled out fur of cat and cur, The
punch - drunk! Be - lieve me, sir, I much pre - fer The
G Gdim7 G
fine mis - mat - ing of a him and her, I've learned my les - son, but I
clas - sic bat - tle of a him and her, I don't like qui - et and I
B7 Em Am7 D7
1
G Am7 D7
2
G Am7 G
wish I were in love a - gain! The
wish I were in love a - gain!

IMAGINE

Words by LORENZ HART
Music by RICHARD RODGERS

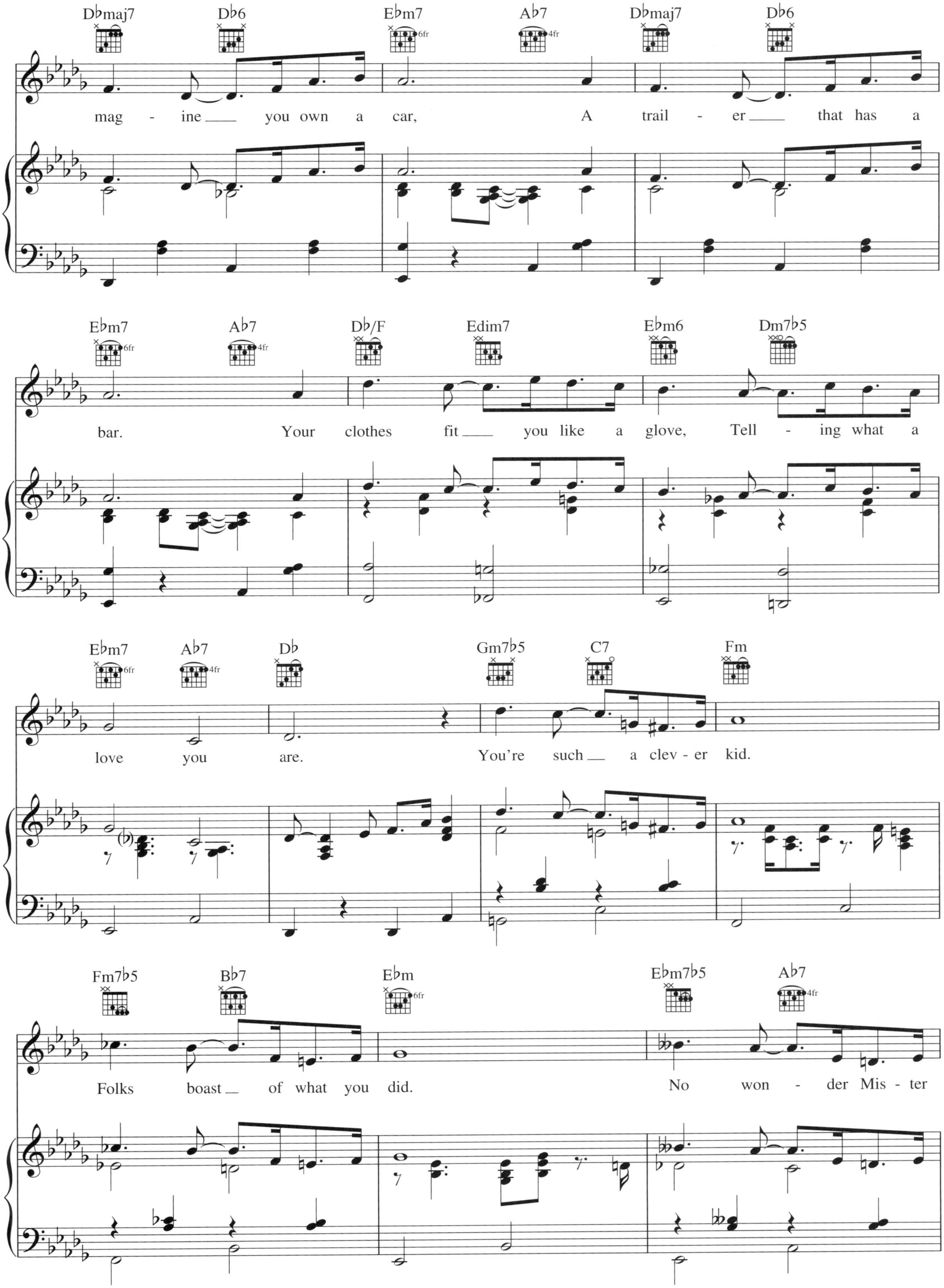

D♭maj7 D♭6 E♭m7 A♭7 D♭maj7 D♭6

mag - ine you own a car, A trail - er that has a

E♭m7 A♭7 D♭/F Edim7 E♭m6 Dm7♭5

bar. Your clothes fit you like a glove, Tell - ing what a

E♭m7 A♭7 D♭ Gm7♭5 C7 Fm

love you are. You're such a clev - er kid.

Fm7♭5 B♭7 E♭m E♭m7♭5 A♭7

Folks boast of what you did. No won - der Mis - ter

D♭ Fm7/C B♭m7 E♭7 A7♭5 A♭7 A♭7♯5 D♭maj7 D♭6
Gold - wyn made a bid. I - mag - ine you're out of
E♭m7 A♭7 D♭maj7 D♭6 E♭m7 A♭7
debt And love brings you no re - gret. If
D♭/F Edim7 E♭m6 Dm7♭5 E♭m7 A♭7 D♭
you can i - mag - ine this, Then you must be nuts, my pet.
rit.
Freely
Gm7♭5 C7 Fm Fm7♭5 B♭7
You're Broad - way's bright - est star, Lights light up where you

Tempo I
E♭m
E♭m7♭5
A♭7
N.C.
D♭
N.C.
Fm7
N.C.
B♭m7
N.C.
E♭7
are. You're more_ di-vine than e - ven Gret - a
A7♭5
A♭7
D♭maj7
D♭6
E♭m7
A♭7
Gar - bo._ I - mag - ine_ at sev - en - teen, You're
D♭maj7
D♭6
E♭m7
A♭7
D♭/F
Edim7
queen of_ the nar - row screen. If you can_ i - mag - ine
E♭m6
Dm7♭5
N.C.
E♭m7
N.C.
A♭7
N.C.
D♭
this, You_ should hit the couch, old bean.

JOHNNY ONE-NOTE

Words by LORENZ HART
Music by RICHARD RODGERS

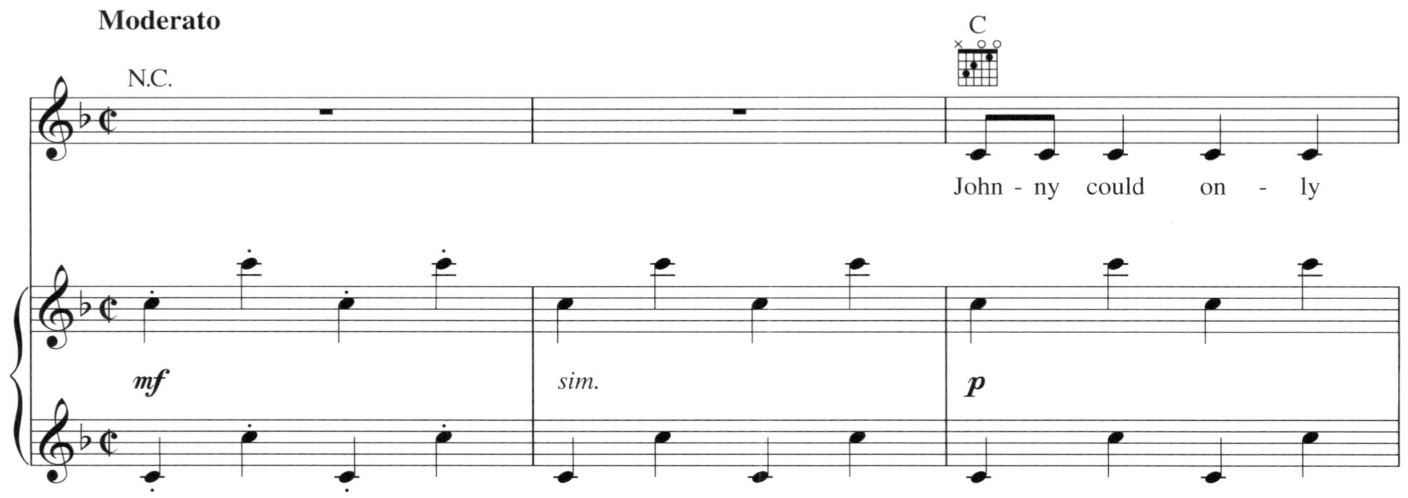

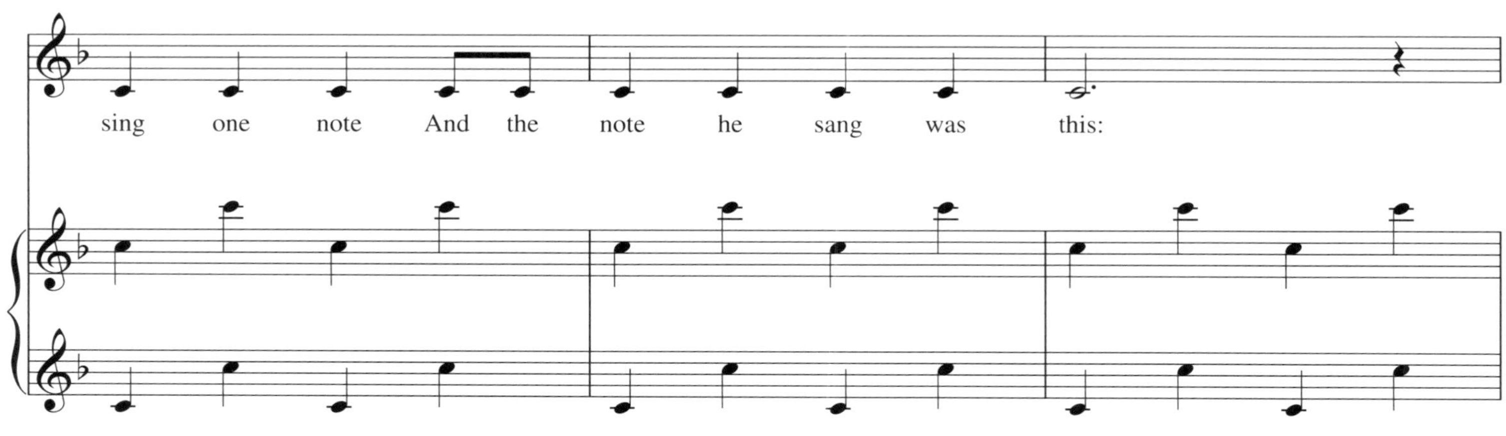

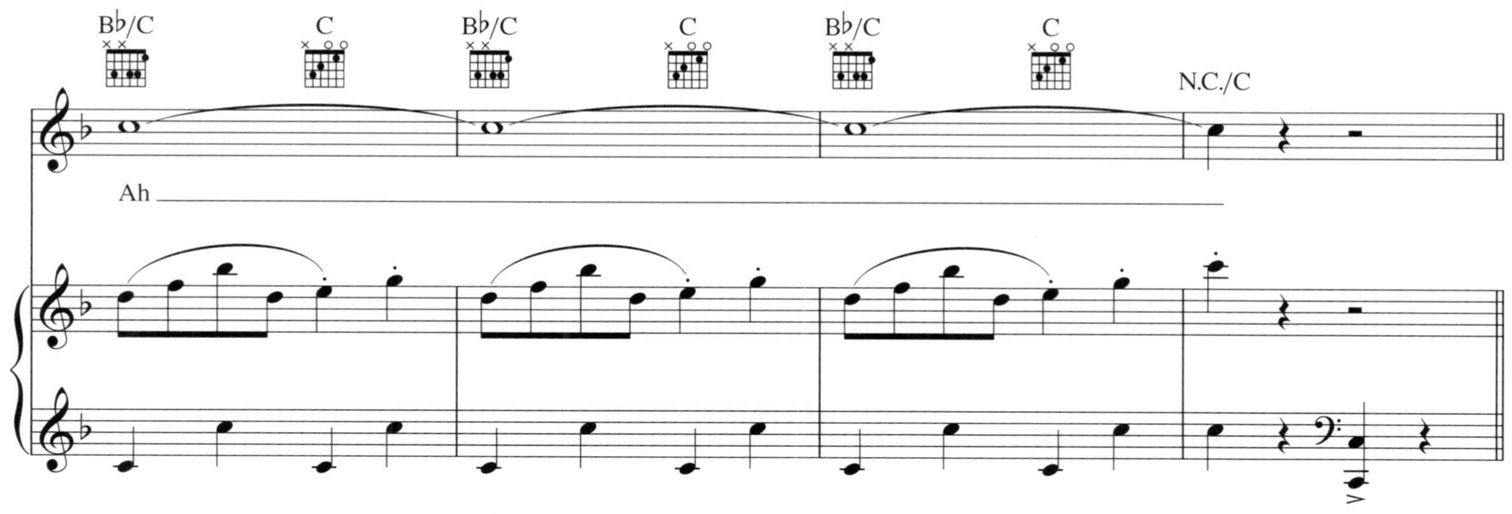

Brightly
F C7 F F6 C7
Poor John - ny One - Note Sang out with gus - to And
F F6 C7 F Fmaj7 Gm7 C7
just o - ver - lord - ed the place.
F C7 F F6 C7
Poor John - ny One - Note Yelled wil - ly - nil - ly, Un -
F F6 C7 D9 4fr D7 Gm7
til he was blue in the face, For

F Gm7 C7 F Fmaj7
hold - ing one note was his ace. Could - n't hear the
A♭ 4fr C7/G F Fmaj7
brass, Could - n't hear the drum, He was in a
A♭ 4fr C7/G F F6 C13 2fr
class By him - self, by gum!
F C7 F F6 C7
Poor John - ny One - Note Got in A - i - da, In -

F F6 C7 F Fmaj7 Gm7 C7
deed a great chance to be brave.
F C7 F F6 C7
He took his one note, Howled like the North Wind, Brought
F F6 C7 D9 4fr D7 Gm7
forth wind that made crit - ics rave, While
F Gm7 C7 F Fmaj7
Ver - di turned round in his grave! Could - n't hear the

A♭
C7/G
F
Fmaj7
flute or the big trom - bone. Ev - 'ry - one was
A♭
C7/G
F
N.C./C
mute, John - ny stood a - lone.
8va
Fm
C7
B♭m/C
C7
Fm
B♭/C
C7
B♭/C
Cats and dogs stopped yap - ping, Li - ons in the zoo all were
C7
B♭/C
C7
B♭/C
C7
B♭
Fm
C7
jeal - ous of John - ny's big trill.

Fm
C7
B♭m/C
C7
Fm
B♭/C
C7
B♭/C
Thun - der - claps stopped clap - ping, Traf - fic ceased its roar, and they
C7
B♭/C
C7
B♭/C
C7
Fm
tell us Ni - ag - 'ra stood still. He stopped the
C/G
F/G
C/G
F/G
train whis - tles, Boat whis - tles, Steam whis - tles, Cop whis - tles;
C7/G
Ddim7/G
C
B♭
Am/C
C7
All whis - tles bowed to his skill.

F
C7
F
F6
Sing John - ny One - Note,
Sing out with
C7
F
F6
C7
gus - to And just o - ver - whelm all the
F
Fmaj7
Gm7
C7
F
C7
crowd.
Ah!
F
F6
C7
F
F6
C7

D9
4fr
D7
Gm7
F
Gm7
C7
So sing, John - ny One - Note, out
loud!
Sing, John - ny One - Note!
Sing, John - ny
cresc.
Gm
3fr
One - Note, out loud!
rit.
f marcato

THE LADY IS A TRAMP

Words by LORENZ HART
Music by RICHARD RODGERS

E9
E7
A7
D9
4fr
D7
las, I missed the Beaux Arts Ball and what is twice as
G7
G+
3fr
C
Am
F
G7
sad, I was nev - er at a par - ty where they
C
G+
3fr
Em7♭5
A7♭9
5fr
D7
hon - ored No - el Ca - 'ad. But so - cial cir - cles
Dm7/C
Em/B
F/C
Em/G
Dm/F
D7
spin too fast for me,
My
L.H.

G7 Eb F/G Em/G B/G G7
3fr
Ho - bo - he - mia is the place to be.
C Cm7 Dm7 G7
3fr
I get too hun - gry For din - ner at eight,
mf
C Cm7 Dm7 G7
3fr
I like the thea - tre but nev - er come late.
C Cmaj7 C9 F Dm7b5
I nev - er both - er with peo - ple I hate,

C/G
E+
F
G7
C
G7
That's why the la - dy is a tramp.
C
Cm7
3fr
Dm7
G7
I don't like crap games With Bar - ons and Earls,
C
Cm7
3fr
Dm7
G7
Won't go to Har - lem In er - mine and pearls
C
Cmaj7
C9
F
Dm7♭5
Won't dish the dirt with the rest of the girls,

C/G
E+
F
G7
C
F/G
C
That's why the la - dy is a tramp.
I like the
Fmaj7
G13/F
Em7
Am
free fresh wind in my hair,
Dm7
G13
C
A7
Life with - out care.
I'm broke,
D9
G7
C
Cm7
it's oke,
Hate Cal - i - for - nia, It's
p

Dm E7 Bm7♭5 E7 Am Am(maj7) Am7

cold and it's damp, That's why the

1

D7 G7 C Am Dm7 G7

la - dy is a tramp.

cresc. ***mf***

2

D7 A♭7♯11 3fr G7 C Cmaj7

la - dy is a tramp.

cresc. ***f***

Cm7 3fr Dm/C Fm/C G7 C

MY FUNNY VALENTINE

Words by LORENZ HART
Music by RICHARD RODGERS

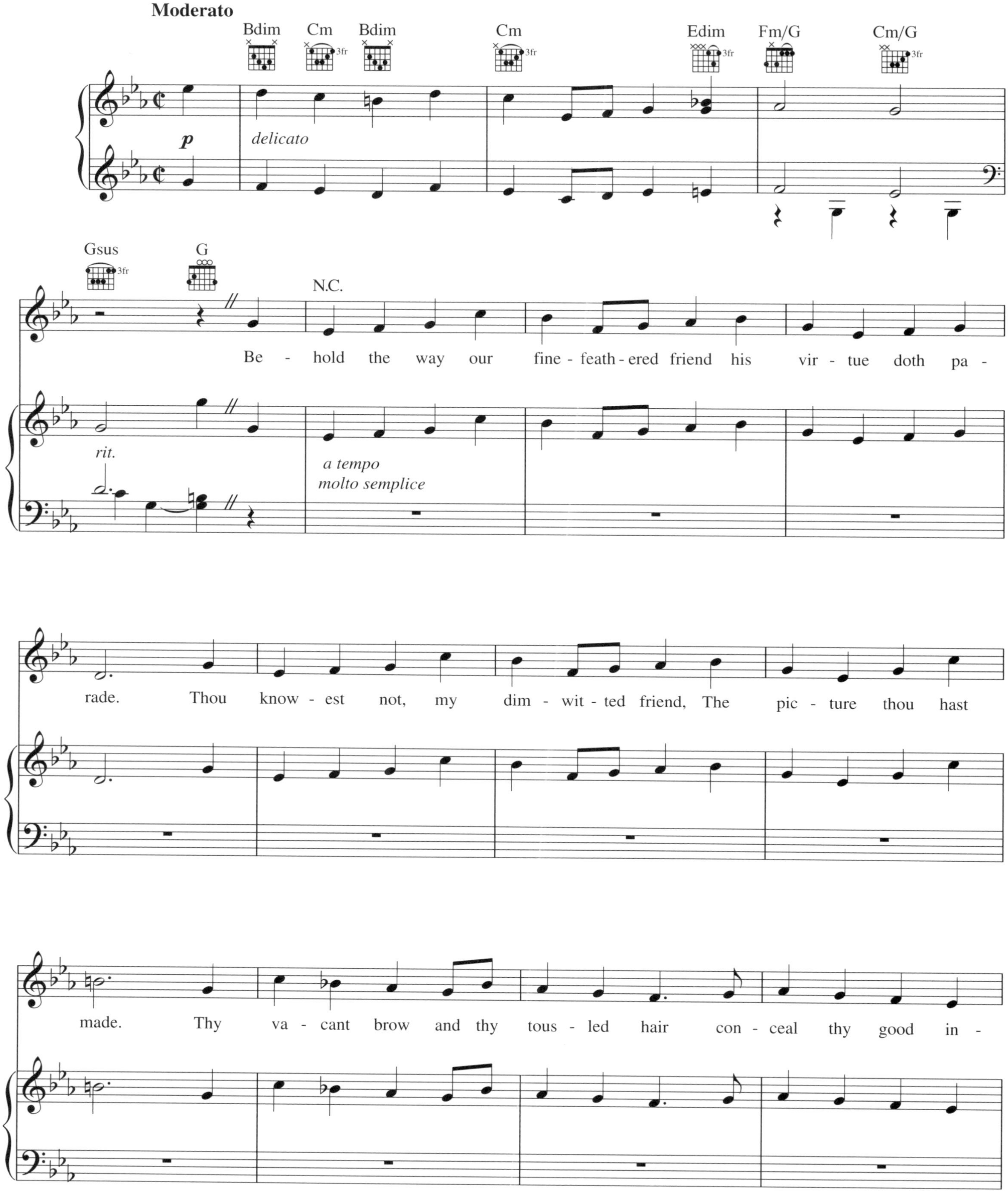

Moderato

Bdim Cm Bdim Cm Edim Fm/G Cm/G

p *delicato*

Gsus G N.C.

Be - hold the way our fine - feath - ered friend his vir - tue doth pa -

rit. *a tempo* *molto semplice*

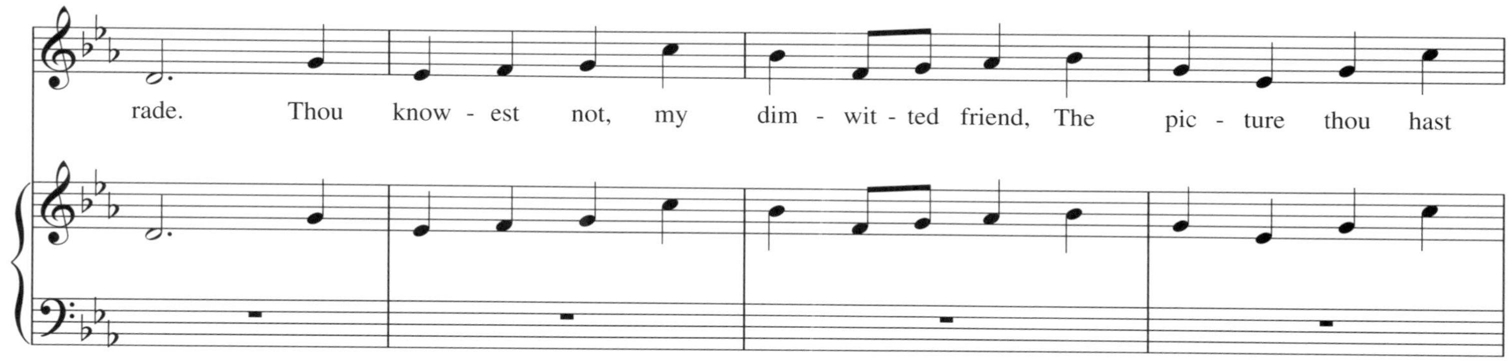

tent. Thou no - ble, up - right, truth - ful, sin - cere and slight - ly dop - ey
Slowly, with much expression
G7♯5
Cm
3fr
G7/C
Cm7
3fr
gent, you're My fun - ny Val - en - tine, Sweet com - ic
p
Cm6
3fr
A♭/C
Fm7
Val - en - tine, You make me smile with my
Dm7♭5
G7
Fm/A♭
G7
Cm
3fr
G7/C
heart. Your looks are laugh - a - ble,

Cm7
3fr
Cm6
3fr
A♭/C
Un - pho - to - graph - a - ble, Yet, you're my
Fm7
Fm7♭5
B♭7
B♭7/A♭
E♭/G
3fr
B♭sus/F
B♭7
fav - 'rite work of art. Is your fig - ure less than
E♭/G
3fr
B♭sus/F
B♭7
E♭6/G
3fr
B♭sus/F
B♭7
E♭/G
3fr
B♭sus/F
B♭7
E♭maj7/G
G7♯5
G7
Greek; Is your mouth a lit - tle weak, when you o - pen it to
Cm
3fr
A♭maj7
A♭6
3fr
A♭7
4fr
G7
Cm
3fr
speak, Are you smart? But don't change a

G7/C
Cm7
3fr
Cm6
3fr
hair for me, Not if you care for me,
A♭/C
A♭7♯11
3fr
G7
Cm
3fr
E♭7
Stay, lit - tle Val - en - tine, stay!
A♭
4fr
A♭/G
Fm7
B♭7
1
E♭
3fr
Each day is Val - en - tine's day.
A♭7
4fr
G7
2
E♭6
day.

WHERE OR WHEN

Words by LORENZ HART
Music by RICHARD RODGERS

Cm7
F7
B♭7
E♭7
B♭7
E♭7
A♭
lived be - fore All that you live to - day. Things you do
Fm7
Fm7♭5
Fm7/B♭
B♭7
E♭
come back to you, As though they knew the way Oh, the
With tender expression
Fm
B♭7
E♭
E♭6
tricks your mind can play! It seems we stood and talked like
poco rit.
E♭maj7
Fm7/E♭
this be - fore. We looked at each oth - er in the

same way then, But I can't re - mem - ber where or
Ebmaj7
3fr
Eb6
Fm7b5
Bb7
Eb
3fr
when.
The clothes you're
Eb6
Ebmaj7
3fr
Fm7/Eb
wear - ing are the clothes you wore. The smile you are smil - ing you were
smil - ing then, But I can't re - mem - ber where or

E♭maj7
3fr
E♭6
Dm7♭5
G7
Cm
3fr
when.
Some things that
Fm7
G7sus
G7
F/G
G7
hap - pen for the first time,
Cm
3fr
Fm7
F7sus
F7
Seem to be hap - pen - ing a - gain.
Fm7/B♭
B♭7
E♭
3fr
E♭6
And so it seems that we have

E♭maj7 E♭+/G Fm/A♭

met be - fore, and laughed be -

Gm/B♭ Fm/A♭ Gm

fore, and loved be - fore, But

Fsus Fm B♭13 B♭7 1 E♭ E♭maj7 Fm/E♭ E♭maj7

who knows where or when!

Fm/E♭ B♭7sus B♭7 2 E♭ A♭m6 C♭ E♭

when!

rit.

YOU'RE NEARER

Words by LORENZ HART
Music by RICHARD RODGERS

B♭m7
E♭7
A♭maj7
D♭maj7
G♭
G♭/F
low, Pre - cious as the sun to the things that grow.
E♭m7
A♭7♯5(♭9)
D♭(add2)
D♭
D♭maj7
D♭6
E♭m7
A♭7
You're near - er than the i - vy to the wall is.
E♭m7
A♭7
D♭/F
E♭7
A♭7
F7/C
Near - er than the win - ter to the fall is.
F7
B♭m7
E♭7
D♭/A♭
Leave me, but when you're a - way you'll

G♭m6
D♭/F
E♭m7
A♭7
know You're near - er, for I love you
p
D♭
Edim/A♭
E♭m7
A♭7♯5(♭9)
so. You're
dim.
pp
2
Slower, broadly
B♭m7
Leave me,
mf
E♭7
E♭13
E♭7♭9
D♭/A♭
G♭m6
but when you're a - way you'll know You're
Freely
D♭
Ddim
E♭m7
A♭7
D♭
E♭9/D♭
G♭dim/D♭
D♭
near - er, for I love you so.
mp
dim. e rall.
pp